Other Translations by David Hinton

The Mountain Poems of Hsieh Ling-yün

Tao Te Ching

The Selected Poems of Po Chü-i The Analects

Mencius

The Late Poems of Meng Chiao

The Selected Poems of Li Po

The Selected Poems of T'ao Ch'ien

The Selected Poems of Tu Fu

TAO TE CHING

Lao Tzu

Translated by David Hinton

COUNTERPOINT NEW YORK

First paperback edition 2002

Library of Congress Cataloging-in-Publication Data
Lao Tzu.
[Tao te ching. English]
Tao Te Ching / Lao Tzu ; translated by David Hinton.
p. cm.
ISBN 1-58243-182-5
I. Hinton, David, 1954– . II. Title.
BL1900.L3 E5 2000
299'.51482–dc21   00–022551
                              CIP

Printed in the United States of America on acid-free
paper that meets the American National Standards Insti-
tute Z39-48 Standard.

Illustration: Nine Dragons (detail), China, Southern Sung
dynasty, dated 1244; Ch'en Jung, Chinese (active first half
of the 13th century) Handscroll; ink and touches of red on
paper; H x L: 18³⁄₁₆ x 431¹¹⁄₁₆ in. Francis Gardner Curtis
Fund, 17.1697.

Design and electronic production by David Bullen Design

COUNTERPOINT
387 Park Avenue South
New York, NY 10016-8810

Counterpoint is a member of the Perseus Books Group.

Contents

Introduction

In the realm of ancient Chinese myth, earth's generative natural process takes the awesome form of dragon. Both feared and revered as the mysterious force of life itself, dragon animates all things in the unending cycle of life and death and rebirth. As it embodies the process of change itself, dragon appears only to disappear again, and so is in constant transformation. Its scales glisten in the bark of rain-swept pines, and it roams seething waters. It descends into deep pools and lakes in autumn, where it hibernates until spring, when its awakening is the awakening of spring and the return of life to earth. It rises from the depths and ascends into the sky, its voice filling the spring winds that scatter autumn leaves. It takes the shape of storm clouds, its claws becoming lightning, and produces the life-bringing spring rains.

Throughout the millennial turning of this seasonal process, spirituality in ancient China was primarily a matter of dwelling at the deepest levels of our belonging to dragon's realm. And this spiritual ecology traces its source back to the origins of Taoist thought: to the sage antics of Chuang Tzu and beyond, to the dark ambiguities and evocative silences of Lao Tzu's mysterious poetry. Indeed, after his legendary encounter with Lao Tzu, an awestruck Confucius exclaimed: "A dragon mounting wind and cloud to soar through the heavens – such things are beyond me. And today, meeting Lao Tzu, it was like facing a dragon."

The question of the historical Lao Tzu is itself a case study in dragon's protean nature. Centuries before the first scraps of Lao Tzu's legend coalesced, he had already vanished into the scattered fragments that eventually evolved into the little book that now bears his name. In the cultural legend, Lao Tzu was an elder contemporary of Confucius (551-479 B.C.E.). But in spite of his stature as a sage, nothing verifiable is known about him, and even the cultural legend is made up of very few facts: he was born in the state of Ch'u and became a court archivist in the Chou capital; he was consulted by Confucius, who emerged from the meeting awestruck; he left the world, heartsick at the ways of people, and as he was going through a mountain pass to vanish into the far west, the gatekeeper there convinced him to leave behind his five-thousand-word scroll of wisdom.

The actual biography of the *Tao Te Ching*'s author, whose name simply means "Old Master," no doubt looks quite different. He was probably constructed out of fragments gleaned from various old sage-masters active between perhaps the sixth and fourth centuries B.C.E., at the historical beginnings of Chinese philosophy. These early texts were worn away, broken up, scattered, assembled, and reassembled: a geologic process lasting several hundred years that apparently included a number of sage editors who wove this material into the single enduring voice that we find in the *Tao Te Ching*. The result of this rather impersonal process was a remarkably personal presence: if we look past the fragmentary text and oracular tone,

•

we find a voice that is consistent and compassionate, unique and rich with the complexities of personality.

It seems likely that a good deal of the material woven into Lao Tzu's voice actually predates the historical beginnings of Chinese philosophy, deriving from an ancient oral tradition. The sayings themselves may predate Lao Tzu by three centuries, but the origins of this oral tradition must go back to the culture's most primal roots, to a level early enough that a distinctively Chinese culture had yet to emerge, for the philosophy of Tao embodies a cosmology rooted in that most primal and wondrous presence: earth's mysterious generative force. This force must have been truly wondrous to those primal people not only because of the unending miracle of new life seemingly appearing from nothing, but also because that miracle was so vital to their well-being, providing them with food, water, clothing, shelter, and of course, a future in their children.

In the Paleolithic, the human experience of the mystery of this generative force gave rise to such early forms of human art as vulvas etched into stone and female figures emphasizing the sense of fecundity. This art was no doubt associated with the development of humankind's earliest spiritual practices: the various forms of obeisance to a Great Mother who continuously gives birth to all creation, and who, like the natural process which she represents, also takes life and regenerates it in an unending cycle of life, death, and rebirth. These phenomena appear to be ubiquitous among later Paleolithic and early Neolithic cultures, where they are integral to gynocentric and egalitarian social structures.

In the *Tao Te Ching,* this venerable generative force appears most explicitly in Lao Tzu's recurring references to the female principle (see Key Terms: *mu,* etc.), such as: "mother of all beneath heaven," "nurturing mother," "valley spirit," "dark female-enigma." But its dark mystery is everywhere in the *Tao Te Ching,* for it is nothing other than Tao itself, the central concept in Lao Tzu's thought. It is a joy to imagine that the earliest of the sages woven into Lao Tzu, those responsible for the core regions of his thought, were in fact women from the culture's proto-Chinese Paleolithic roots.

The primal generative process revered by those earliest of Chinese sages takes on new dimensions in Lao Tzu's Tao, dimensions that carry it into realms we now speak of as ontology and ecology, cosmology, phenomenology, and social philosophy. *Tao* originally meant "way," as in "pathway" or "roadway," and Lao Tzu recast it as a spiritual Way by using it to describe that inexplicable generative force seen as an ongoing process (hence a "Way"). This Way might be provisionally described as a kind of generative ontological process through which all things arise and pass away, and Lao Tzu's way is to dwell as a part of that natural process. In that dwelling, self is but a fleeting form taken on by earth's process of change. Or more absolutely, it is all and none of earth's fleeting forms simultaneously: that is, it is pure dragon.

The story of this dragon has endured for nearly 2500 years now in the voice of Lao Tzu, and as such it has been the defining spiritual way in China. Once your eyes become adjusted to the strange light in the world of this Old Master's teachings, you learn to see yourself inside Ch'en Jung's grand dragon painting (interior illustration). There, a young dragon just appearing from shadowy mist and cloud is being taught by a sage old dragon – its mane thin and white, its teeth half gone, its body fading back into mist and cloud.

Lao Tzu's thought is driven by a sense of exile that derives from a fundamental rupture between human being and natural process. During the Paleolithic, humans began to be aware of themselves as separate from natural process, and the distance that this separation opened allowed the generative-centered worldview to arise. This intermediary stage, where humans were still rooted in natural process and yet separate enough to produce a rich artistic and spiritual tradition, continued into the agrarian cultures of the early Neolithic. But for a number of reasons the separation eventually became a rupture as Neolithic humans in agrarian villages began "controlling nature" in the form of domesticated plants and animals. This process coincides with a shift from the gynocentric worldview to an androcentric worldview. Although he lacked a precise anthropological understanding of human evolution, Lao Tzu often alludes to this historical process, always with disdain. And indeed, at one point he reduces this monumental transformation to a single poetic image: "When all beneath heaven forgets Way, / war horses are bred among the fertility altars" (46.3-4).

In China, this rupture had become a complete separation by the historical beginnings of Chinese civilization in the Shang Dynasty (1766-1040 B.C.E.), which marked the transition from Neolithic to Bronze Age culture and was already fiercely patriarchal. The Shang was preceded by the Neolithic Hsia Dynasty, about which very little is known. But it appears that in the Paleolithic cultures that preceded the Hsia, another spiritual practice developed alongside the reverent celebration of the Great Mother, another reflection of how deeply humans felt their belonging to earth as a whole: nature deities were worshiped as tribal ancestors. Hence a tribe may have traced its lineage back to an originary "High Ancestor River," for instance. This practice apparently survived through the Hsia into the Shang, where evidence of it appears in oracle-bone inscriptions. These nature deities continued to be worshiped in their own right; but within the ideology of power, religious life focused on the worship of human ancestors, all male.

By forging this new religious system into a powerful form of theocratic government, the Shang was able to dominate Chinese civilization for no less than seven hundred years. The Shang emperors ruled by virtue of their lineage, which was sanctified by Shang Ti ("Celestial Lord"), a supreme deity who functioned as the source of creation, order, ethics, etc. The Shang house may even have traced its lineage directly back to Shang Ti as its originary ancestor. (*Shang* here represents two entirely different words in Chinese.) In any case, Shang Ti provided the Shang rulers with a transcendental source of legitimacy and power: he protected and advanced their interests, and through their spirit-ancestors, they could decisively influence Shang Ti's shaping of events. All aspects of people's lives were thus controlled by the emperor: weather, harvest, politics, economics, religion, etc. Indeed, people didn't experience themselves as substantially different from spirits, for the human realm was simply an extension of the spirit realm.

This represents a complete reversal from the proto-Chinese worldview: feminine to masculine, nurturing to dominating, body to spirit, earthly to heavenly. The Paleolithic unity of human and natural process has become a complete rupture in this worldview, which is very like that of the Judeo-Christian West in its fundamental outlines: a monotheism in which spiritual connections locate the human in a transcendental spirit realm rather than the tangible earthly realm.

Such was the imperial ideology, convenient to the uses of power because it accorded little ethical value to the masses not of select lineages. (Not surprisingly, the rise of Shang Ti seems to coincide with the rise of the Shang Dynasty, and later myth speaks of him as the creator of Shang civilization.) In the cruelest of ironies, it was overwhelming human suffering that brought the Chinese people back into their earthly lives, beginning the transformation of this spiritualistic culture back to a humanistic one. In the cultural legend, the early Shang rulers were paradigms of nobility and benevolence. But by the end of the Shang, the rulers had become cruel and tyrannical, and as there was no ethical system separate from the religious system, there was nothing to shield the people from their depredations. Meanwhile, a small nation was being pushed to the borders of the Shang realm by western tribes. This state of "semi-barbarian" people, known as the Chou, gradually adopted the cultural traits of the Shang. Eventually, under the leadership of the legendary sage-emperors Wen ("cultured") and Wu ("martial"), the Chou overthrew the tyrannical Shang ruler, thus founding the Chou Dynasty (1040-223), which was welcomed wholeheartedly by the Shang people.

The Chou conquerors were faced with an obvious problem: if the Shang lineage had an absolute claim to rule the world, how could the Chou justify replacing it with their own, and how could they legitimize their rule in the eyes of the Shang people? Their solution was to reinvent Shang Ti in the form of heaven, thus ending the Shang's claim to legitimacy by lineage, and then proclaim that the right to rule depended upon the Mandate of Heaven: once a ruler becomes unworthy, heaven withdraws its mandate and bestows it on another. This was a major event in Chinese philosophy: the first investment of power with an ethical imperative. And happily, the early centuries of the Chou appear to have fulfilled that imperative admirably.

But eventually the Chou foundered, both because of its increasing inhumanity and its lack of the Shang's transcendent source of legitimacy: if the Mandate could be transferred to the Chou, it could obviously be transferred again. The rulers of the empire's component states grew increasingly powerful, claiming more and more sovereignty over their lands, until finally they were virtually independent nations. Eventually these rulers (properly entitled "dukes") even began assuming the title of emperor, thus equating themselves with the Chou emperor, who was by now a mere figurehead. The rulers of these autonomous states could at least claim descent from those who were first given the territories by the early Chou rulers. But this last semblance of legitimacy was also crumbling because power was being usurped by a second tier of local lords whenever they had the strength to take it, and even a third tier of high officials serving in the governments of usurping dukes and lords. This history, beginning with the

Chou's overthrow of the Shang, represents a geologic split in China's social structure: political power was breaking free of its family/religious context and becoming a separate entity.

The final result of the Chou's "metaphysical" breakdown was, not surprisingly, all too physical: war. In addition to constant pressure from "barbarians" in the north (the first devastating blow to Chou power was a "barbarian" invasion in 770) and the "semi-barbarian" Ch'u realm that dominated south China, there was relentless fighting between the empire's component states and frequent rebellion within them. This internal situation, devastating to the people, continued to deteriorate after Lao Tzu's time, until it finally gave an entire age its name: the Warring States Period (403-221). Meanwhile, rulers caught up in this ruthless competition began looking for the most able men to help them rule their states, and this precipitated the rise of an independent intellectual class – a monumental event, for this class constituted the first open space in the cultural framework from which the imperial ideology could be challenged. The old spiritualist social order had now collapsed entirely, and these intellectuals began struggling to create a new one. Although this was one of the most virulent and chaotic periods in Chinese history, it was the golden age of Chinese philosophy, for there were a "Hundred Schools of Thought" trying to envision what this new social order should be like. These schools were founded by thinkers who wandered the country with their disciples, teaching and trying to convince the various rulers to put their ideas into practice, for the desperate times had given them an urgent sense of political mission.

Confucius was the first great figure in this independent intellectual class, China's first self-conscious philosopher who can be historically verified in any sense, and Lao Tzu may be spoken of as his elder contemporary in terms of both the cultural legend and the development of early Chinese thought. Lao Tzu's appearance at that crucial moment in Chinese history certainly looks very much like the awakening dragon revitalizing a civilization in which the life-force had dwindled to a mere flicker. Formulated in the ruins of a magisterial monotheism that had dominated China for a millennium, a situation not at all unlike that of the modern West, Lao Tzu's Way initiated the transformation of early China's otherworldly spiritualist culture to an earthly humanist culture founded on a spirituality of our immediate empirical experience: our belonging to the realm of dragon.

Although its inexplicable nature is a central motif in the *Tao Te Ching*, we might approach Lao Tzu's Way by speaking of it at its deep ontological level, where the distinction between being and nonbeing arises. Being can be understood provisionally in a fairly straightforward way as the empirical world, earth's ten thousand things in constant transformation; and nonbeing as the generative void from which being arises. Within this framework, Way can be understood as the process of nonbeing continuously generating the realm of being. But Lao Tzu's descriptions of Way in its more mysterious aspect as nonbeing tend to the poetic and paradoxical: he speaks of it as "emptiness," "silence," and "dark-enigma." And here we are quickly cast adrift in the realm of unknowing at the heart of Lao Tzu's thought, for in its essential nature as nonbeing, where it precedes the differentiation of the ten thousand things, Way also precedes the differentiation of language itself. Indeed, *Tao* doesn't necessarily capture what Lao Tzu is describing at all: he says that he doesn't know its name, that he's only calling it *Tao*.

The ontological structure of Way is replicated in the structure of human consciousness, thoughts arising from the same generative emptiness as the ten thousand things. Hence, Way is utterly inexplicable for it quite literally precedes thought. Lao Tzu says that being and nonbeing give birth to one another: they are one and the same, but once they arise, they differ in name. And there before they arise, where they remain one and the same, is the Way beyond all differentiation.

It is here in the depths of consciousness that Way can be experienced directly through the practice of meditation. You can watch the process of Way as thought burgeons forth from the emptiness and disappears back into it, or you can simply dwell in that undifferentiated emptiness, that generative realm of nonbeing. With this meditative dwelling in the emptiness of nonbeing, you are at the heart of Lao Tzu's spiritual ecology, reinhabiting the primal universe in the most profound way. Here where the distinction between subjectivity and objectivity dissolves, consciousness and natural process blend into a single tissue. And no doubt a part of what makes meditation so profound an experience is that it frees us from our most fundamental dislocation, for it has only been in the last few thousand years that human consciousness has experienced itself as separate from natural process. So in returning us to the undifferentiated levels of consciousness and ontology, meditative practice returns us to the ancient undifferentiated levels of human culture.

Taoism was eventually supplemented and intensified by Ch'an (Zen) Buddhism, which is a melding of Taoism and Buddhism. Ch'an became widely influential beginning in the T'ang Dynasty (618-907 C.E.) – but Taoism continued as the defining spiritual Way, for its insight remained vital not only in Taoism itself, but also in the essential core of Ch'an practice. And nothing is more essential to Ch'an practice than meditation: indeed, *ch'an* literally means "meditation." The practice of meditation is not discussed extensively in early Taoist literature as it is in Ch'an literature. But it is clear that such meditation was practiced, for the *Tao Te Ching* and *Chuang Tzu* both contain a number of passages that allude to the meditative experience. Not surprisingly, references by Lao Tzu the poet tend to be oblique: in fact, a good deal of the text can be read as describing meditative awareness as the texture defining a sage's every action. Where not oblique or implicit, the references appear in the form of poetry rather than discursive description: "Can you polish the dark-enigma mirror / to a clarity beyond stain?" (10.5-6), "Inhabit the furthest peripheries of emptiness / and abide in the tranquil center" (16.1-2), "sitting still in Way's company" (62.10),

> Block the senses
> and close the mind,
> blunt edges,
> loosen tangles,
> soften glare,
> mingle dust:
> this is called *dark-enigma union.*
>
> (56. 3-9)

And perhaps the most impressive aspect of Lao Tzu's power as a poet is how his poetic strategies induce this meditative experience in the reader. Mysterious utterances, misty terminology, fragmentary collage form with open and enigmatic juxtapositions, an abounding ambiguity that exploits the uncertainty inherent to the syntax and semantics of ancient Chinese – these surprisingly modern strategies all keep the poetry as close as possible to the undifferentiated primal mystery of Way, forcing the reader to participate in the generative emptiness at the source of language, mind, and all heaven and earth.

In the context of Lao Tzu's cosmology as a whole, the realm of being takes on depths beyond our provisional definition of it as the empirical world around us. In the lexicon of early Taoist texts, *heaven* is a near synonym for *Way* – though it focuses on these depths in the region of being, while *Way* tends to focus on the mysterious region of nonbeing. A term that already had a considerable historical resonance when Lao Tzu and Chuang Tzu adopted it and made it their own, *heaven's* most primitive meaning is simply "sky." By extension, it also comes to mean "transcendence," for our most primal sense of transcendence may be the simple act of looking up into the sky. By association with the idea of transcendence and that which is beyond us, *heaven* also comes to mean "fate" or "destiny." But this unsurprising complex of ideas is transformed completely when early Taoism adds "nature" or "natural process" to the weave of meaning, for then heaven becomes earth, and earth heaven. Earth's natural process is itself both our fate in life and our transcendence, for self is but a fleeting form taken on by earth's process of change – born out of it, and returned to it in death. Or more precisely, never *out of it:* totally unborn. Our truest self, being unborn, is all and none of earth's fleeting forms simultaneously.

Not surprisingly, given the apparent antiquity of Lao Tzu's entire cosmology, this unborn perspective seems to have survived from very ancient times in the deep levels of Chinese consciousness, indeed the term *(shen)* meaning "self" meant at the same time "body." However ancient it may be, it is a philosophical statement of a principle central to the modern science of ecology – that the earth's biota is a complex food web and we humans are as much a part of it as any other organism. And in the interim between early China and modern science, this unborn perspective became an enduring source of great solace for the Chinese educated class, not least when confronting their own mortality. They recognized in it a kind of immortality, as Lao Tzu suggests a number of times, and they experienced this unborn perspective routinely in the texture of consciousness. Just as the body dissolves back into the generative process at death, they could watch the movements of self (thought, emotion) dissolve back into the generative source, and there meditatively inhabit that perennial death.

Lao Tzu's heaven represents the endpoint in a millennium-long evolution of mythological thought. He and Chuang Tzu used it to both secularize the sacred and to invest the secular with sacred dimensions. Lao Tzu begins a new tradition free of the dichotomy between secular and sacred in the concept of *tzu-jan,* which is virtually synonymous with heaven but without heaven's transcendental baggage. *Tzu-jan*'s literal meaning is "self-so" or "the of-itself," which as a philosophical concept becomes "being such of itself," hence "spontaneous" or "natural." But a more revealing translation of *tzu-jan* might be "occurrence appearing of itself," for it is meant to describe the ten thousand things burgeoning forth spontaneously from the generative source, each according to its own nature, independent and self-sufficient, each dying and returning to the process of change, only to reappear in another self-generating form. Again it is striking how this most primal of worldviews is also utterly modern, for it accords with the science of ecology both in its description of how living systems work as integral wholes and in its attention to the particularity of each individual within the system.

Mythologies are stories about *tzu-jan,* but Lao Tzu returned to occurrence free of myth. This clarity may well derive from the primal oral tradition that persisted outside the mythological power structures of the Shang and Chou, but in any case it represents a return to the same proto-Chinese cultural levels where experience was organized around obeisance to earth's generative force. *Tzu-jan* is nothing other than the earth seen as a boundless generative organism, and this vision gives rise to a very different experience of the world. Rather than the metaphysics of time and space, this experience knows the world as an all-encompassing present, a constant burgeoning forth of something we might now call *spacetime.* Or more precisely, it is a constant transformation in things, for its burgeoning forth stretches out to include what we think of as past and future: like Lao Tzu's Way, it makes no distinction between filling and emptying; hence passing away is as much a part of it as coming to be. In this burgeoning forth, there is also no distinction between subjective and objective, for it includes all that we call mental, all that appears in the mind. And here lies the awesome sense of the sacred in this generative world: each of the ten thousand things, consciousness among them, seems to be miraculously burgeoning forth from a kind of emptiness at its own heart, and at the same time it is always a burgeoing forth from the very heart of the Cosmos itself.

The antiquity of this cosmology may be reflected in the conspicuous absence of a central creation myth in historical China (not surprisingly, it seems such a myth did exist in the Shang), for in such a cosmology there can be no single primordial creation of the world: its creation is an ongoing total event. But in China this cosmology is perhaps most fundamentally alive in the language itself, and its presence there at such deep levels is yet another indication that its origins go back to the earliest cultural levels, levels where culture and language were just emerging, characters just emerging from hieroglyphs. It is alive in the minimal grammar, where meaning is determined simply by the order in which words occur in an open field where much of the ordering human presence is absent, and alive in the immediate physicality of the pictographic nouns and verbs. But it is especially alive in the verbs: rather than embodying a metaphysics of time and space, rather than events in a flow of past, present, and future, the uninflected verbs of ancient Chinese simply register action, that steady burgeoning forth of occurrence appearing of itself. And even in the more articulated grammar of modern Chinese, verbs simply register completed action and action: occurrence and occurrence appearing of itself.

The Taoist Way is to dwell as an organic part of this bur-geoning forth by practicing *wu-wei* (see Key Terms), another central term which literally means "doing nothing" in the sense of not interfering with the flawless and self-sufficient un-folding of *tzu-jan*. But this must always be conceived together with its mirror image: "nothing doing" or "nothing's own doing," in the sense of being no one separate from *tzu-jan* when acting. *Wu-wei* is the movement of *tzu-jan*, so when we act according to *wu-wei* we act as the generative source. This opens to the deepest level of this philosophical complex, for *wu-wei* can also be read quite literally as "nonbeing *(wu)* doing." And this in turn invests the more straightforward reading ("doing nothing") with its fullest dimensions, for "doing noth-ing" always carries the sense of "enacting nothing/nonbeing." Thus it might be described as a return to the primal dwelling of the generative worldview.

The principle of *wu-wei* raises the question of Te (Integrity), the other key word in this book's title: *Tao (Way) Te (Integrity) Ching (Classic)*, or *The Classic of the Way and Integrity (to the Way)*. Te involves integrity to the Way in the sense of "abiding by the Way," or "enacting the Way." For the "nonhuman natu-ral world," Te is not a problem because the ten thousand trans-formations are wholly *wu-wei*. Only in the human realm is the Integrity of *wu-wei* problematic. Here we encounter the sense of exile that drives much of Lao Tzu's thought, that rupture dividing human being and natural process. While Western civ-ilization set out headlong into the barrens of that exile, China returned and stayed close to its lost homeland, cultivating the rich borderlands.

As humans no longer simply belong to natural process, that belonging was carefully cultivated in the form of *wu-wei* and a more general intimacy with the nonhuman "natural world." Rooted in Lao Tzu's spiritual ecology, these practices became the very terms of self-cultivation throughout the centuries in China. This is most clearly seen in artistic practice, which was a major part of intellectual life for everyone in the educated class, and nothing less than a form of spiritual discipline: calligraphers, poets, and painters aspired to create with the selfless spontaneity of a natural force, and the elements out of which they crafted their artistic visions were primarily aspects of the "natural world:" moon and stars, rivers and mountains, fields and gardens. But it can also be seen, for instance, in the way Chinese intellectuals would sip wine as a way of dissolving the separation between self and "natural world," a practice that usually took place outdoors or in an architectural space that aspired to be a kind of eye-space, its open walls creating an emptiness that contained the world around it. There is a host of other examples, such as the ideal of living as a recluse among the mountains, or meditation which was widely practiced and recognized as perhaps the most fundamental form of *wu-wei* belonging to natural process.

And so it is that Lao Tzu's Way has defined the spiritual Way in China. But like the other Hundred-School philosophers, Lao Tzu felt his primary mission was to rescue the ravaged society of his time, and *wu-wei* Integrity is central to his politics, for it also describes the proper functioning of society as a whole for him. Like human consciousness, the structure of this society echoes the ontological structure of Way. The people (like

thoughts) take the place of being's ten thousand things burgeoning forth, each according to its own nature. And the
ruler/government (like empty mind) takes the place of nonbeing, simply providing the empty field in which citizens can
burgeon forth, each according to their own nature. Hence, he
returns society to a state where it functions with the same *wu-
wei* Integrity to Way as any other natural process. Lao Tzu's
ideal society is essentially an early Neolithic generative-centered culture, though he conceived it as a kind of monarchy,
for that was the only political system known or even imagina-
ble in ancient China. But Lao Tzu's is a monarchy in name
only, for his ideal monarch is virtually invisible.

Like all Chinese, Lao Tzu believed such a society was once
the norm: the cultural legend describes society in the era pre-
ceding the Hsia Dynasty in these terms and includes a list of
its sage-emperors. Lao Tzu believed that since those early
times, society had crumbled as people lost their primal sense
of belonging to the generative process of Way. Rather than
acting with the simple naturalness of the human animal, they
had become driven by self-aggrandizing pursuits: that is, the
pursuit of desires beyond "natural" needs such as food, shelter, sex, etc. These "unnatural" desires for wealth and status
and power transform an egalitarian society into a virulent web
of dominance and submission, where the enhancement of a
few comes at great cost to the many. In fact, this is exactly the
historical process that began in the Neolithic. And it goes without saying that Lao Tzu's critique represents a fundamental critique of modern capitalism, thriving as it does on fabricating
desire.

Lao Tzu's Way to a rich and harmonious society is for people to follow *wu-wei* Integrity, to satisfy needs but forget desires. This political critique of desire echoes the more fundamental critique of desire at the levels where consciousness and ontology merge. Even the least act of desire, saying *yes this* and *no that*, places us outside the spontaneous generative process. Accepting whatever comes of *tzu-jan* is to return to the undifferentiated source in ontology and consciousness. This is the same movement as society's return to *wu-wei* Integrity, and is no doubt its prerequisite. All of these are included when Lao Tzu speaks of "returning to Way." In all three aspects (politics, ontology, consciousness), it is a return to the earliest undifferentiated levels of human culture – levels so early they precede difference altogether, meaning such societies are not only radically egalitarian, but that issues of ethics and social justice hadn't even arisen yet.

Lao Tzu's political philosophy is a logical extension of his ontology – not only replicating its structure, but also replicating its profound subjectivity as a kind of uncompromising individualism. And this is in itself a radical and enduring politics. Still, however accurate and appealing his idealistic vision may be, it had little to offer as a practical prescription for counteracting the ruthless forces that ravage human society, for the simple reason that it fundamentally contradicts the principle of Way. Having associated desire with being and said such things as "desire drives change," Lao Tzu knew perfectly well that natural process is itself the boundless form of desire, the ten thousand things pushing beyond themselves through one transformation after another. And humans are a part of those transformations: whatever we do, whatever desires drive us, that too is part of Way. Indeed, as Lao Tzu must have been thinking when he spoke of Way as indifferent and inhumane, even as "the Executioner," the so-called harmony of natural process includes a great deal of waste and destruction. Lao Tzu's prescription for solving social injustice was itself a colossal system of "unnatural" desire, a hopeless attempt to change the most fundamental makeup of not only the human world, but of Way itself.

Chuang Tzu was the more consistent and thoroughgoing Taoist. Realizing that developments in human society, however tragic, were a natural part of Way, he made no attempt to forge Taoist thought into a system of social justice. Indeed, his was a wholesale rejection of the human-centered approach. But although Lao Tzu shared this rejection, he was driven by a profound compassion. Here is the beautiful and compelling humanity of Lao Tzu: his concern for the desperate plight of common people drove him to advocate political principles that contradicted the fundamental terms of his philosophy. And the inevitable failure of these contradictory principles no doubt led to the frustration and hopelessness that drove Lao Tzu over the pass and away into the west. In the end, his is not so much a practical political philosophy as a political poetry, a lament that only grows more and more poignant as stratified societies continue to thrive on social injustice.

While the Way of philosophical Taoism has defined the private spiritual realm for Chinese intellectuals throughout the millennia, the Confucian Way has defined the societal realm. Although Lao Tzu longed to apply his wisdom to the social problems of his time, this role fell to Confucius, who created a radically new social system, one that was both consistent with the fundamental terms of Lao Tzu's thought and applicable in a practical way to secular society. In his social philosophy, Confucius seems to be drawing out the implications of a cosmology that already existed in the culture. Rather than a newly created replacement for the Shang monotheism, it seems to have survived from the more primal cultures that preceded the Shang, once again revealing Shang monotheism to be a mere ideological overlay convenient to the uses of power. The resilience of this cosmology after a thousand years of neglect is remarkable and especially interesting as it is so consistent with both our immediate experience and the modern scientific account of the cosmos. In any case, it would appear that the earlier levels of Lao Tzu formulated this cosmology for the Hundred-Schools era, and that Confucius relied on that formulation. So the cosmology that shaped Chinese civilization was the resurgence of an ancient cosmology, a return to the culture's most primal roots, though as Marx would expect, even this gynocentric cosmology could not preclude the workaday male tyranny that has dominated Chinese culture throughout its history (hence the sages of ancient China were men, as in this translation). And it is a return not only to the generative worldview, but also to the general sense of *wu-wei* belonging to natural process as a secular extension of the reverence for ancestral nature deities that also typified proto-Chinese cultures.

With the addition of the political dimensions formulated by Confucius, Lao Tzu's majestic vision became the operant possibility for China's secular society, however rarely it was realized in practice: human being nestled in the primal ecology of a spontaneously self-generating and harmonious cosmos. The two regions of this cosmology appear almost schematically in countless Chinese landscape paintings: the pregnant emptiness of nonbeing, and the landscape of being as it burgeons forth from nonbeing in a perpetual process of transformation. And then, within that cosmology of natural process, there is the human. It was among the vistas of these sparsely peopled landscapes so dramatically burgeoning forth out of vast realms of emptiness that Lao Tzu set out across the mountain pass in Chang Lu's painting (cover illustration): overwhelmed by the intractable grief people were enduring, and yet smiling at a butterfly, Chuang Tzu's famous image for the exquisite and dreamlike transformation of things (end of chapter 2). In leaving through the mountains into dusk-lit mists of the west, Lao Tzu vanished back into that mysterious transformation of things, and the voice that remains is the voice of that mystery herself, the voice of dragon, voice of earth.

Tao Ching

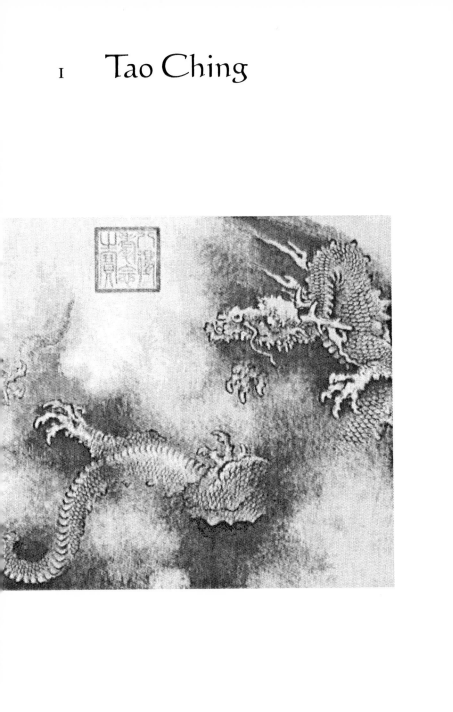

I

A Way become Way isn't the perennial Way.
A name become name isn't the perennial name:

the named is mother to the ten thousand things,
but the unnamed is origin to all heaven and earth.

In perennial nonbeing you see mystery,
and in perennial being you see appearance.
Though the two are one and the same,
once they arise, they differ in name.

One and the same they're called *dark-enigma,*
dark-enigma deep within dark-enigma,

gateway of all mystery.

2

All beneath heaven knows beauty is beauty
only because there's ugliness,
and knows good is good
only because there's evil.

Being and nonbeing give birth to one another,
difficult and easy complete one another,
long and short measure one another,
high and low fill one another,
music and noise harmonize one another,
before and after follow one another:

that's why a sage abides in the realm of nothing's own doing,
living out that wordless teaching.
The ten thousand things arise without beginnings there,
abide without waiting there,
come to perfection without dwelling there.

Without dwelling there: that's the one way
you'll never lose it.

3

Never bestow honors
and people won't quarrel.
Never prize rare treasures
and people won't steal.
Never flaunt alluring things
and people won't be confused.

This is how a sage governs.
Fill bellies and empty minds,
strengthen bones and weaken ambition,

always keep the people from knowing and wanting,
then those who know are those who never presume to act.

If you're nothing doing what you do
all things will be governed well.

4

Way is empty.
Use it: it never needs filling.
An abyss so deep
it seems ancestor to the ten thousand things,

it blunts edges,
loosens tangles,
softens glare,
mingles dust.

A clarity so clear it only seems real,

whose child could it be? Apparently
it precedes gods and creators.

5

Heaven and earth are Inhumane:
they use the ten thousand things like straw dogs.
And the sage too is Inhumane:
he uses the hundred-fold people like straw dogs.

Is all heaven and earth
really so much like a bellows-chamber?
It's empty but never contracts,
just keeps bringing forth more and more.

Words go on failing and failing,
nothing like abiding in its midst.

6

The valley spirit never dies.

It's called *dark female-enigma*,
and the gateway of dark female-enigma
is called *the root of heaven and earth,*

gossamer so unceasing it seems real.
Use it: it's effortless.

7

Heaven goes on forever.
Earth endures forever.

There's a reason heaven and earth go on enduring forever:
their life isn't their own
so their life goes on forever.

Hence, in putting himself last
the sage puts himself first,
and in giving himself up
he preserves himself.

If you aren't free of yourself
how will you ever become yourself?

8

Lofty nobility is like water.
Water's nobility is to enrich the ten thousand things
and yet never strive:
it just settles through places people everywhere loathe.
Therefore, it's nearly Way.

Dwelling's nobility is earth,
mind's nobility is empty depth,
giving's nobility is Humanity,
word's nobility is sincerity,
government's nobility is accord,
endeavor's nobility is ability,
action's nobility is timing.

When you never strive
you never go wrong.

9

Forcing it fuller and fuller
can't compare to just enough,
and honed sharper and sharper
means it won't keep for long.

Once it's full of jade and gold
your house will never be safe.
Proud of wealth and renown
you bring on your own ruin.

Just do what you do, and then leave:
such is the Way of heaven.

10

Can you let your spirit embrace primal unity
without drifting away?

Can you focus *ch'i* into such softness
you're a newborn again?

Can you polish the dark-enigma mirror
to a clarity beyond stain?

Can you make loving the people and ruling the nation
nothing's own doing?

Can you be female
opening and closing heaven's gate?

Can you fathom earth's four distances with radiant wisdom
and know nothing?

Give birth and nurture.
Give birth without possessing
and foster without dominating:

this is called *dark-enigma Integrity.*

II

Thirty spokes gathered at each hub:
absence makes the cart work.
A storage jar fashioned out of clay:
absence makes the jar work.
Doors and windows cut in a house:
absence makes the house work.

Presence gives things their value,
but absence makes them work.

12

The five colors blind eyes.
The five tones deafen ears.
The five tastes blur tongues.
Fast horses and breathtaking hunts make minds wild and crazy.
Things rare and expensive make people lose their way.

That's why a sage tends to the belly, not the eye,
always ignores *that* and chooses *this*.

13

Honor is a contagion deep as fear,
renown a calamity profound as self.

Why do I call honor a contagion deep as fear?
Honor always dwindles away,
so earning it fills us with fear
and losing it fills us with fear.

And why do I call renown a calamity profound as self?
We only know calamity because we have these selves.
If we didn't have selves
what calamity could touch us?

When all beneath heaven is your self in renown
you trust yourself to all beneath heaven,
and when all beneath heaven is your self in love
you dwell throughout all beneath heaven.

14

Looked at but never seen,
it takes the name *invisible*.
Listened to but never heard,
it takes the name *ethereal*.
Held tight but never felt,
it takes the name *gossamer*.

You can't unravel these three
blurred so utterly they've become one,

rising without radiance
and setting without darkness,
braided together beyond name, woven
back always and forever into nothing:

this is called *formless form*
or *nothing's image*,
called *spectral confusion*,

something you meet without seeing a front
and follow without seeing a back.

Abiding in the ancient Way
to master what has now come to be
and fathom its ancient source:

this is called *thread of the Way*.

15

Ancient masters of Way
all subtle mystery and dark-enigma vision:
they were deep beyond knowing,

so deep beyond knowing
we can only describe their appearance:

perfectly cautious, as if crossing winter streams,
and perfectly watchful, as if neighbors threatened;
perfectly reserved, as if guests,
perfectly expansive, as if ice melting away,
and perfectly simple, as if uncarved wood;
perfectly empty, as if open valleys,
and perfectly shadowy, as if murky water.

Who's murky enough to settle slowly into pure clarity,
and who still enough to awaken slowly into life?

If you nurture this Way, you never crave fullness.
Never crave fullness
and you'll wear away into completion.

16

Inhabit the furthest peripheries of emptiness
and abide in the tranquil center.

There the ten thousand things arise,
and in them I watch the return:
all things on and ever on
each returning to its root.

Returning to the root is called *tranquility,*
tranquility is called *returning to the inevitable unfolding of things,*
returning to the inevitable unfolding of things is called *constancy,*
and to understand constancy is called *enlightenment.*

Without understanding constancy, you stumble deceived.
But understanding constancy, you're all-embracing,

all-embracing and therefore impartial,
impartial and therefore imperial,
imperial and therefore heaven,
heaven and therefore Way,
Way and therefore enduring:

self gone, free of danger.

17

The loftiest ruler is barely known among those below.
Next comes a ruler people love and praise.
After that, one they fear,
and then one they despise.

If you don't stand sincere by your words
how sincere can the people be?
Take great care over words, treasure them,

and when the hundred-fold people see
your work succeed in all they do
they'll say it's just *occurrence appearing of itself.*

18

When the great Way is abandoned
we're faced with Humanity and Duty.

When clever wisdom appears
we're faced with duplicity.

When familial harmony ends
we're faced with obedience and kindness.

And when chaos engulfs the nation
we're faced with trustworthy ministers.

19

If you give up sagehood and abandon wisdom
people will profit a hundred times over.

If you give up Humanity and abandon Duty
people will return to obedience and kindness.

If you give up ingenuity and abandon profit
bandits and thieves will roam no more.

But these three
are mere refinements, nowhere near enough.
They depend on something more:

observe origin's weave, embrace uncarved simplicity,
self nearly forgotten, desires rare.

20

If you give up learning, troubles end.

How much difference is there
beween yes and no?
And is there a difference
between lovely and ugly?

If we can't stop fearing
those things people fear,
it's pure confusion, never-ending confusion.

People all radiate such joy,
happily offering a sacrificial ox
or climbing a tower in spring.
But I go nowhere and reveal nothing,
like a newborn child who has yet to smile,
aimless and worn out
as if the way home were lost.

People all have enough and more.
But I'm abandoned and destitute,
an absolute simpleton, this mind of mine so utterly
muddled and blank.

Others are bright and clear:
I'm dark and murky.
Others are confident and effective:
I'm pensive and withdrawn,

uneasy as boundless seas
or perennial mountain winds.

People all have a purpose in life,
but I'm inept, thoroughly useless and backward.
I'll never be like other people:
I keep to the nurturing mother.

21

The nature of great Integrity
is to follow Way absolutely.

Becoming things, Way appears
vague and hazy.
All hazy and impossibly vague
it harbors the mind's images.
All vague and impossibly hazy
it harbors the world's things.

All hidden and impossibly dark
it harbors the subtle essence,
and being an essence so real
it harbors the sincerity of facts.

Never, not since the beginning—
its renown has never been far off.
Through it we witness all origins.

And how can we ever know the form of all origins?
Through this.

.

•

22

In yielding is completion.
In bent is straight.
In hollow is full.
In exhaustion is renewal.
In little is contentment.
In much is confusion.

This is how a sage embraces primal unity
as the measure of all beneath heaven.

Give up self-reflection
and you're soon enlightened.
Give up self-definition
and you're soon apparent.
Give up self-promotion
and you're soon proverbial.
Give up self-esteem
and you're soon perennial.
Simply give up contention
and soon nothing in all beneath heaven contends with you.

It was hardly empty talk
when the ancients declared *In yielding is completion*.
Once you perfect completion
you've returned home to it all.

23

Keeping words spare: occurrence appearing of itself.

Wild winds never last all morning
and fierce rains never last all day.
Who conjures such things if not heaven and earth,
and if heaven and earth can't make things last,
why should we humans try?

That's why masters devote themselves to Way.
To master Way is to become Way,
to master gain is to become gain,
to master loss is to become loss.
And whatever becomes Way, Way welcomes joyfully,
whatever becomes gain, gain welcomes joyfully,
whatever becomes loss, loss welcomes joyfully.

If you don't stand sincere by your words
how sincere can the people be?

24

Stretch onto tiptoes
and you never stand firm.
Hurry long strides
and you never travel far.

Keep up self-reflection
and you'll never be enlightened.
Keep up self-definition
and you'll never be apparent.
Keep up self-promotion
and you'll never be proverbial.
Keep up self-esteem
and you'll never be perennial.

Travelers of the Way call such striving
too much food and useless baggage.
Things may not all despise such striving,
but a master of the Way stays clear of it.

25

There was something all murky shadow,
born before heaven and earth:

o such utter silence, utter emptiness.

Isolate and changeless,
it moves everywhere without fail:

picture the mother of all beneath heaven.

I don't know its name.
I'll call it *Way*,
and if I must name it, name it *Vast*.

Vast means it's passing beyond,
passing beyond means it's gone far away,
and gone far away means it's come back.

Because Way is vast
heaven is vast,
earth is vast,
and the true emperor too is vast.
In this realm, there are four vast things,
and the true emperor is one of them.

Human abides by earth.
Earth abides by heaven.
Heaven abides by Way.
Way abides by occurrence appearing of itself.

26

Heavy is the root of light,
and tranquil the ruler of reckless.

A sage traveling all day
is never far from the supplies in his cart,
and however spectacular the views
he remains calm and composed.

How can a lord having ten thousand chariots
act lightly in governing all beneath heaven?
Act lightly and you lose your source-root.
Act recklessly and you lose your rule.

27

Perfect travels leave no tracks.
Perfect words leave no doubts.
Perfect accounts need no counting.
Perfect gates close without locks
and so cannot be opened.
Perfect knots bind without rope
and so cannot be loosened.

A sage is always perfect in rescuing people
and so abandons no one,
always perfect in rescuing things
and so abandons nothing.

This is called the *bequest of enlightenment,*

so one who possesses this perfection is a teacher of those who don't,
and those who don't possess it are the resource of one who does.

Without honoring the teacher
and loving the resource,
no amount of wisdom can prevent vast confusion.

This is called *the essential mystery.*

28

Knowing the masculine
and nurturing the feminine
you become the river of all beneath heaven.
River of all beneath heaven
you abide by perennial Integrity
and so return to infancy.

Knowing the white
and nurturing the black
you become the pattern of all beneath heaven.
Pattern of all beneath heaven
you abide by perennial Integrity
and so return to the boundless.

Knowing splendor
and nurturing ruin
you become the valley of all beneath heaven.
Valley of all beneath heaven
you rest content in perennial Integrity
and so return to the simplicity of uncarved wood.

When uncarved wood is split apart
it becomes mere implements.
But when a sage is employed
he becomes a true minister,
for the great governing blade carves nothing.

29

Longing to take hold of all beneath heaven and improve it . . .
I've seen such dreams invariably fail.
All beneath heaven is a sacred vessel,
something beyond all improvement.
Try to improve it and you ruin it.
Try to hold it and you lose it.

For things sometimes lead and sometimes follow,
sometimes sigh and sometimes storm,
sometimes strengthen and sometimes weaken,
sometimes kill and sometimes die.

And so the sage steers clear of extremes,
clear of extravagance,
clear of exhaltation.

.

•

30

If you use the Way to help a ruler of people
you never use weapons to coerce all beneath heaven.
Such things always turn against you:

fields where soldiers camp
turn to thorn and bramble,
and vast armies on the march
leave years of misery behind.

The noble prevail if they must, then stop:
they never press on to coerce the world.

Prevail, but never presume.
Prevail, but never boast.
Prevail, but never exult.
Prevail, but never when there's another way.
This is to prevail without coercing.

Things grown strong soon grow old.
This is called *losing the Way:*
Lose the Way and you die young.

31

Auspicious weapons are the tools of misfortune.
Things may not all despise such tools,
but a master of the Way stays clear of them.

The noble-minded treasure the left when home
and the right when taking up weapons of war.

Weapons are tools of misfortune,
not tools of the noble-minded.
When there's no other way,
they take up weapons with tranquil calm,
finding no glory in victory.

To find glory in victory
is to savor killing people,
and if you savor killing people
you'll never guide all beneath heaven.

We honor the left in celebrations
and honor the right in lamentations,
so captains stand on the left
and generals on the right.
But use them both as if conducting a funeral:

when so many people are being killed
it should be done with tears and mourning.
And victory too should be conducted like a funeral.

32

Way is perennially nameless,
an uncarved simplicity. Though small,
it's subject to nothing in all beneath heaven.
But when lords or emperors foster it,
the ten thousand things gladly become their guests,

heaven mingling with earth
sends down sweet dew,
and the people free of mandates
share justice among themselves.

When a governing blade begins carving it up, names arise.
Once names arise,
know that it's time to stop.
Knowing when to stop, you can avoid danger.

Way flowing through all beneath heaven:
it's like valley streams flowing into rivers and seas.

33

To know people is wisdom,
but to know yourself is enlightenment.

To master people takes force,
but to master yourself takes strength.

To know contentment is wealth,
and to live with strength resolve.
To never leave whatever you are
is to abide,
and to die without getting lost—
that is to live on and on.

34

Way is vast, a flood
so utterly vast it's flowing everywhere.

The ten thousand things depend on it:
giving them life and never leaving them
it performs wonders but remains nameless.

Feeding and clothing the ten thousand things
without ruling over them,
perennially that free of desire,
it's small in name.
And being what the ten thousand things return to
without ruling over them,
it's vast in name.

It never makes itself vast
and so becomes utterly vast.

35

Holding to the great image
all beneath heaven sets out:
sets out free of risk,
peace tranquil and vast.

Music and savory food
entice travelers to stop,
but the Way uttered forth
isn't even the thinnest of bland flavors.

Look at it: not enough to see.
Listen to it: not enough to hear.
Use it: not enough to use up.

36

To gather
you must scatter.
To weaken
you must strengthen.
To abandon
you must foster.
To take
you must give.
This is called *dusky enlightenment*.

Soft and weak overcome hard and strong.

Fish should be kept in their watery depths:
a nation's honed instruments of power
should be kept well-hidden from the people.

37

Way is perennially doing nothing
so there's nothing it doesn't do.

When lords and emperors abide by this
the ten thousand things follow change of themselves.

Desire drives change,
but I've stilled it with uncarved nameless simplicity.

Uncarved nameless simplicity
is the perfect absence of desire,
and the absence of desire means repose:
all beneath heaven at rest of itself.

Te Ching

38

High Integrity never has Integrity
and so is indeed Integrity.
Low Integrity never loses Integrity
and so is not at all Integrity.

High Integrity does nothing
and has no motives.
Low Integrity does something
and has sure motives.
High Humanity does something
and has no motives.
High Duty does something
and has sure motives.
High Ritual does something,
and when no one follows along
it rolls up its sleeves
and forces them into line.

Lose Way, and Integrity appears.
Lose Integrity, and Humanity appears.
Lose Humanity, and Duty appears.
Lose Duty, and Ritual apppears.

Ritual is the thinning away of loyalty and sincerity,
the beginning of chaos,
and prophecy is the flowery semblance of Way,
the beginning of folly.

This is why a great elder
inhabits thick rather than thin,
fruitful substance rather than flowery semblance,

always ignores *that* and chooses *this*.

39

Ancients who realized primal unity:

Heaven realized primal unity
and so came to clarity.
Earth realized primal unity
and so came to tranquility.
Gods realized primal unity
and so came to spirit.
Valleys realized primal unity
and so came to fullness.
The ten thousand things realized primal unity
and so came to life.
Lords and emperors realized primal unity
and so came to rectify all beneath heaven.

It's their very existence:
without clarity heaven cracks open,
without tranquility earth bursts forth,
without spirit gods cease,
without fullness valleys run dry,
without life the ten thousand things perish,
without high nobility lords and emperors stumble and fall.

Nobility is rooted in humility,
and high founded on low.
This is why true lords and emperors call themselves
orphaned, destitute, ill-fated.
Isn't this rooted in humility?
Isn't it

counting the world's praise as no praise,
refusing to tinkle like delicate jade bells
or clatter like ponderous stone chimes?

•

•

40

Return is the movement of Way,
and yielding the method of Way.

All beneath heaven, the ten thousand things: it's all born of being,
and being is born of nonbeing.

41

When the lofty hear of Way
they devote themselves.
When the common hear of Way
they wonder if it's real or not.
And when the lowly hear of Way
they laugh out loud.
Without that laughter, it wouldn't be Way.

Hence the abiding proverbs:

Luminous Way seems dark.
Advancing Way seems retreating.
Formless Way seems manifold.

High Integrity seems low-lying.
Great whiteness seems tarnished.
Abounding Integrity seems lacking.
Abiding Integrity seems missing.
True essence seems protean.

The great square has no corners,
and the great implement completes nothing.
The great voice sounds faint,
and the great image has no shape.

Way remains hidden and nameless,
but it alone nourishes and brings to completion.

42

Way gave birth to one,
and one gave birth to two.
Two gave birth to three,
and three gave birth to the ten thousand things.
Then the ten thousand things shouldered *yin* and embraced *yang*,
blending *ch'i* to establish harmony.

People all hate scraping by
orphaned, destitute, ill-fated,
but true dukes and emperors call themselves just that.

Some things gain by loss,
and some lose by gain.

I only teach
what the people teach:
Tyranny and force never come to a natural end.
I've taken the people as my schoolmaster.

43

The weakest in all beneath heaven gallops through the strongest,
and vacant absence slips inside solid presence.

I know by this the value of nothing's own doing.

The teaching without words,
the value of nothing's own doing:
few indeed master such things.

44

Name or self: which is precious?
Self or wealth: which is treasure?
Gain or loss: which is affliction?

Indulge love and the cost is dear.
Keep treasures and the loss is lavish.

Knowing contentment you avoid tarnish,
and knowing when to stop you avoid danger.

Try it and your life will last and last.

45

Great perfection seems flawed,
but its usefulness never falters.
Great fullness seems empty,
but its usefulness never runs dry.

Great rectitude seems bent low,
great skill seems clumsy,
great eloquence seems quiet.

Bustling around may overcome cold,
but tranquility overcomes heat.
Master lucid tranquility
and you'll govern all beneath heaven.

46

When all beneath heaven abides in Way,
fast horses are kept to work the fields.
When all beneath heaven forgets Way,
war horses are bred among the fertility altars.

What calamity is greater than no contentment,
and what flaw greater than the passion for gain?

The contentment of fathoming contentment —
there lies the contentment that endures.

47

You can know all beneath heaven
though you never step out the door,
and you can see the Way of heaven
though you never look out the window.

The further you explore, the less you know.

So it is that a sage knows by going nowhere,
names by seeing nothing,
perfects by doing nothing.

48

To work at learning brings more each day.
To work at Way brings less each day,

less and still less
until you're doing nothing yourself.
And when you're doing nothing yourself, there's nothing you don't do.

To grasp all beneath heaven, leave it alone.
Leave it alone, that's all,
and nothing in all beneath heaven will elude you.

49

A sage's mind is never his own:
he makes the hundred-fold people's mind his mind.

I treat the noble with nobility
and the ignoble too:
such is the nobility of Integrity.
I treat the sincere with sincerity
and the insincere too:
such is the sincerity of Integrity.

A sage dwells within all beneath heaven
at ease, mind mingled through it all.
The hundred-fold people devote their eyes and ears,
but a sage inhabits it all like a child.

50

People born into life enter death.
Constant companion in life
and in death,
this body is the kill-site animating their lives.
And isn't that because
they think life is the fullness of life?

I've heard those who encompass the whole of life
could walk on and on without meeting rhinoceros or tiger,
could charge into armies without feeling shield or sword.
A rhinoceros would find nowhere to gore them,
a tiger nowhere to claw them,
a sword nowhere to slice them.

And isn't that because
for them there's no kill-site?

51

Way gives birth to them
and Integrity nurtures them.
Matter shapes them
and conditions complete them.

That's why the ten thousand things always
honor Way and treasure Integrity.

Honoring Way and treasuring Integrity
isn't obedience to command,
it's occurrence perennially appearing of itself.

Way gives birth to them
and Integrity nurtures them:
it fosters and sustains them,
harbors and succors them,
nourishes and shelters them.

Giving birth without possessing,
animating without subjecting,
fostering without dominating:

this is called *dark-enigma Integrity.*

52

There's a source all beneath heaven shares:
call it the mother of all beneath heaven.

Once you fathom the mother
you understand the child,
and once you understand the child
you abide in the mother,

self gone, free of danger.

If you block the senses
and close the mind,
you never struggle.
If you open the senses
and expand your endeavors,
nothing can save you.

Seeing the small is called *enlightenment*,
and abiding in the gentle *strength*.

Wielding radiance
return to enlightenment,
then you're beyond all harm.

This is the cultivation of constancy.

53

Understanding sparse and sparser still
I travel the great Way,
nothing to fear unless I stray.

The great Way is open and smooth,
but people adore twisty paths:
Government in ruins,
fields overgrown
and graineries bare,

they indulge in elegant robes
and sharp swords,
lavish food and drink,
all those trappings of luxury.

It's *vainglorious thievery*—
not the Way, not the Way at all.

54

Something planted so deep it's never rooted up,
something held so tight it's never stolen away:
children and grandchildren will pay it homage always.

Cultivated in yourself
it makes Integrity real.
Cultivated in your family
it makes Integrity plentiful.
Cultivated in your village
it makes Integrity enduring.
Cultivated in your nation
it makes Integrity abundant.
Cultivated in all beneath heaven
it makes Integrity all-encompassing.

So look through self into self,
through family into family,
through village into village,
through nation into nation,
through all beneath heaven into all beneath heaven.

How can I know all beneath heaven as it is?
Through this.

55

Embody Integrity's abundance
and you're like a vibrant child

hornets and vipers can't bite,
savage beasts can't maul
and fierce birds can't claw,

bones supple and muscles tender, but still gripping firmly.
                    .
Knowing nothing of male and female mingling
and yet aroused:
this is the utmost essence.
Wailing all day without getting hoarse:
this is the utmost harmony.

To understand harmony is called *constancy*,
and to understand constancy is called *enlightenment*.

To enhance your life is called *tempting fate*,
and to control *ch'i* with the mind is called *violence*.

Things grown strong soon grow old.
This is called *losing the Way:*
Lose the Way and you die young.

56

Those who know don't talk,
and those who talk don't know.

Block the senses
and close the mind,
blunt edges,
loosen tangles,
soften glare,
mingle dust:

this is called *dark-enigma union*.

It can't be embraced
and can't be ignored,
can't be enhanced
and can't be harmed,
can't be treasured
and can't be despised,

for it's the treasure of all beneath heaven.

57

You may govern the nation through principle
and lead armies to victory through craft,
but you win all beneath heaven through indifference.

How can I know this to be so?
Through this.

The more prohibitions rule all beneath heaven
the deeper poverty grows among the people.
The more shrewd leaders there are
the faster dark confusion fills the nation.
The more cleverness people learn
the faster strange things happen.
The faster laws and decrees are issued
the more bandits and thieves appear.

Therefore a sage says:
I do nothing
and the people transform themselves.
I cherish tranquility
and the people rectify themselves.
I cultivate indifference
and the people enrich themselves.
I desire nothing
and the people return of themselves to uncarved simplicity.

58

When government is pensive and withdrawn
people are pure and simple.
When government is confident and effective
people are cunning and secretive.

Prosperity springs from calamity
and calamity lurks in prosperity.
Who knows where it will all end

without leaders of principle?
And principle always reverts to sinister trickery,
virtue to depraved sorcery.

People have been confused for such a long long time.

That's why a sage is sharp but never cuts,
austere but never grates,
forthright but never provokes,
bright but never dazzles.

59

To govern people and serve heaven
there's nothing like thrift.
Thrift means *submitting early,*
and submitting early means *storing up Integrity.*

Store up Integrity and nothing is beyond you.
Once nothing is beyond you,
no one knows where it will all end.
Once no one knows where it will end,
you can nurture a nation.

And nurturing the nation's mother too
you can last and last.
This is called *rooted deep and solid,*
the Way of long life and enduring insight.

60

Govern a great nation as you would cook a small fish.

Use Way to rule all beneath heaven
and spirits never become ghosts.
When spirits don't become ghosts,
ghosts do people no harm.
When ghosts do people no harm,
sages do them no harm.

And once humans and ghosts do each other no harm,
they return together to Integrity.

61

A great nation flows down into
the place where all beneath heaven converges,
the female of all beneath heaven.

In its stillness, female lies perpetually low,
and there perpetually conquers male.

A great nation that puts itself below a small nation
takes over the small nation,
and a small nation that puts itself below a great nation
gives itself over to the great nation.

Some lie low to take over,
and some lie low to give over.

A great nation wanting nothing more
than to unite and nurture the people
and a small nation wanting nothing more
than to join and serve the people:
they both succeed in what they want.

Great things lie low and rest content.

62

Way is the mystery of these ten thousand things.

It's a good person's treasure
and an evil person's refuge.
Its beautiful words are bought and sold
and its noble deeds are gifts enriching people.

It never abandons even the evil among us.

When the Son of Heaven is enthroned
and the three dukes installed,
parades with jade discs and stately horses
can't compare to sitting still in Way's company.

Isn't it said that
the ancients exalted this Way because
in it *whatever we seek we find,*
and whatever seeks us we escape?

No wonder it's exalted throughout all beneath heaven.

63

If you're nothing doing what you do,
you act without acting
and savor without savoring,

you render the small vast and the few many,
use Integrity to repay hatred,
see the complexity in simplicity,
find the vast in the minute.

The complex affairs of all beneath heaven are there in simplicity,
and the vast affairs of all beneath heaven are there in the minute.
That's why a sage never bothers with vastness
and so becomes utterly vast.

Easy promises breed little trust,
and too much simplicity breeds too much complexity.
That's why a sage inhabits the complexity of things
and so avoids all complexity.

64

It's easy to embrace the tranquil
and easy to prevent trouble before omens appear.
It's easy for the trifling to melt away
and easy for the slight to scatter away.

Work at things before they've begun
and establish order before confusion sets in,

for a tree you can barely reach around
grows from the tiniest rootlet,
a nine-tiered tower
starts as a basket of dirt,
a thousand-mile journey
begins with a single step.

Work at things and you ruin them;
cling to things and you lose them.

That's why a sage does nothing
and so ruins nothing,
clings to nothing
and so loses nothing.

When people devote themselves to something
they always ruin it on the verge of success.

Finish with the same care you took in beginning
and you'll avoid ruining things.

This is why a sage desires without desire,
never longing for rare treasures,
learns without learning,
always returning to what people have passed by,

helps the ten thousand things occur of themselves
by never presuming to work at them.

65

Ancient masters of Way
never enlightened people.
They kept people simple-minded.

It's impossible to govern
once you've filled people with knowing.
Use knowing to govern
and you plunder the nation,
but use not-knowing to govern
and you enrich the nation.

Once you understand this, the pattern is clear,
and always understanding the pattern is called *dark-enigma Integrity*.

Dark-enigma Integrity is deep and distant,
is the return of things

back into the vast harmony.

66

Oceans and rivers become emperors of the hundred valleys
because they stay so perfectly below them.
This alone makes them emperors of the hundred valleys.

So, wanting to rule over the people
a sage speaks from below them,
and wanting to lead the people
he follows along behind them,

then he can reign above without weighing the people down
and stay ahead without leading the people to ruin.

All beneath heaven rejoices in its tireless praise of such a sage.
And because he's given up contention,
nothing in all beneath heaven contends with him.

67

People throughout all beneath heaven say
my Tao is so vast it's like nothing at all.
But it's only vast because it's like nothing at all:
if it were like anything else
it would have long since become trifling.

There are three treasures
I hold and nurture:
The first is called *compassion,*
the second *economy,*
and the third *never daring to lead all beneath heaven.*

Courage comes of compassion,
generosity comes of economy,
and commanding leadership comes of never daring to lead all
        beneath heaven.

But these days it's all courage without compassion,
generosity without economy,
and leading without following.
There's nothing but death in that.

To overcome, attack with compassion.
To stand firm, defend with compassion.
Whatever heaven sustains
it shelters with compassion.

68

A noble official is never warlike,
and a noble warrior is never angered.
A noble conqueror never faces an enemy,
and a noble leader stays below the people he wields.

This is called *the Integrity of peacefulness,*
the power of wielding the people,

the fullest extent of our ancient accord with heaven.

.

•

69

There was once a saying among those who wielded armies:
I'd much rather be a guest than a host,
much rather retreat a foot than advance an inch.

This is called *marching without marching,*
rolling up sleeves without baring arms,
raising swords without brandishing weapons,
entering battle without facing an enemy.

There's no greater calamity than dishonoring an enemy.
Dishonor an enemy and you'll lose those treasures of mine.

When armies face one another in battle,
it's always the tender-hearted one that prevails.

70

My words are so simple to understand
and so easily put into practice
that no one in all beneath heaven understands them
and no one puts them into practice.

Words have their ancestral origins
and actions their sovereign:

it's only because people don't understand this
that they don't understand me.
And the less people understand me
the more precious I become.

So it is that a sage wears sackcloth,
keeping pure jade harbored deep.

71

Knowing not-knowing is lofty.
Not knowing not-knowing is affliction.

A sage stays free of affliction.
Just recognize it as affliction
and you're free of it.

72

When the people stop fearing the fearsome
something truly fearsome will descend upon them.

Don't hem them in
and choke their lives with oppression.
That's all. Just let them be,
and they'll never tire of you.

A sage sees through himself without revealing himself,
loves himself without exalting himself,

always ignores *that* and chooses *this*.

73

To infuse daring with courage means death.
To infuse caution with courage means life.
The one enriches you, and the other ruins you.

No one knows why heaven
despises what it despises,
that's why a sage inhabits the complexity of things.

The Way of heaven never contends
and so overcomes perfectly,
never speaks
and so answers perfectly,
never summons
and so arrives of itself,
stays calm
and so plans perfectly.

The net of heaven is vast, woven so vast
and wide open nothing slips through.

74

In their misery, the people no longer fear death,
so how can you threaten them even with death?

Let the people fear death always,
then if we seize those who follow sinister ways
and put them to death,
no one will dare live such lives.

The Executioner's killing is perennial, it's true.
But to undertake the killing yourself—
that's like trying to carve lumber for a master carpenter.
Try to carve lumber for a master carpenter
and you'll soon have blood on your hands.

75

The people are starving,
and it's only because you leaders feast on taxes
that they're starving.

The people are impossible to rule,
and it's only because you leaders are masters of extenuation
that they're impossible to rule.

The people take death lightly,
and it's only because you leaders crave life's lavish pleasures
that they take death lightly,

they who act without concern for life:
it's a wisdom far beyond treasuring life.

76

People are soft and weak in life,
hard and strong in death.
The ten thousand plants and trees are soft and frail in life,
withered and brittle in death.

Things hard and strong follow death's ways
and things soft and weak follow life's:

so it is that strong armies never overcome
and strong trees always suffer the axe.

Things great and strong dwell below.
Things soft and weak dwell above.

77

The Way of heaven is like a drawn bow
pulling down the high
and raising up the low:

it takes away where there's abundance
and restores where there's want.

The Way of heaven takes away where there's abundance
and restores where there's want,
but the Way of humankind isn't like that:
it takes away where there's want
and gives where there's abundance.

Only a master of the Way
can give abundance to all beneath heaven.
Such a sage acts without presumption
and never dwells on success:

great worth has no need to be seen.

78

Nothing in all beneath heaven is so soft and weak as water.
And yet, for conquering the hard and strong,
nothing succeeds like water.

And nothing can change it:
weak overcoming strong,
soft overcoming hard.
Everything throughout all beneath heaven knows this,
and yet nothing puts it into practice.

That's why the sage said:
Whoever assumes a nation's disgrace
is called the sacred leader of a country,
and whoever assumes a nation's misfortune
is called the emperor of all beneath heaven.

Words of clarity sound confused.

79

You can resolve great rancor,
but rancor always lingers on.

Understanding the more noble way,
a sage holds the creditor's half of contracts
and yet asks nothing of others.
Those with Integrity tend to such contracts;
those without Integrity tend to the collection of taxes.

The Way of heaven is indifferent,
always abiding with people of nobility.

80

Let nations grow smaller and smaller
and people fewer and fewer,

let weapons become rare
and superfluous,
let people feel death's gravity again
and never wander far from home.
Then boat and carriage will sit unused
and shield and sword lie unnoticed.

Let people knot ropes for notation again
and never need anything more,

let them find pleasure in their food
and beauty in their clothes,
peace in their homes
and joy in their ancestral ways.

Then people in neighboring nations will look across to each other,
their chickens and dogs calling back and forth,

and yet they'll grow old and die
without bothering to exchange visits.

81

Sincere words are never beautiful
and beautiful words never sincere.
The noble are never eloquent
and the eloquent never noble.
The knowing are never learned
and the learned never knowing.

A sage never hoards:

the more you do for others
the more plenty is yours,
and the more you give to others
the more abundance is yours.

The Way of heaven is to profit without causing harm,
and the Way of a sage to act without contending.

Notes

The *Tao Te Ching* is traditionally divided into two parts: *Tao Ching (The Classic of Way)* and *Te Ching (The Classic of Integrity)*.

1   **heaven and earth:** For heaven, see Key Terms: t'ien. Given Lao Tzu's cosmology, heaven and earth might be conceived as "creative force and created objects."

Lines 5-6 are an especially noteworthy instance of the rich linguistic ambiguity in ancient Chinese and how well Lao Tzu exploits that potential, for it is often read:

> Free of perennial desire, you see mystery,
>
> and full of perennial desire, you see appearance.

dark-enigma: See Key Terms: *hsüan*.

2   **nothing's own doing:** See Key Terms: *wu-wei*.

4   **gods and creators:** Specifically: Shang Ti, supreme deity of the Shang Dynasty. See Introduction p. xii.

5   **Inhumane:** see note to section 8 below.

straw dogs: offerings used during sacrifices (and then discarded).

8   **Humanity:** Humanity *(jen)* is the touchstone of Confucian virtue. Simply stated, it means to act with a selfless and reverent concern for the well-being of others. See my translation of *The Analects*, pp. xxxiv and 247.

10 **spirit . . . drifting away:** It was generally believed that a person's spirit drifts away after death.

ch'i: The universal breath, vital energy, or life-force.

mirror: mind or pure awareness.

heaven's gate: gateway through which the ten thousand things come into being and return to nothing.

17   **stand sincere by your words:** Typically translated as "sincerity" or "trust," *hsin* sometimes appears in this translation as "standing by words" to reflect its full philosophical dimensions and the etymology so apparent visually in the two elements of its graph, where a person is shown beside words (sounds coming out of a mouth): 信

occurrence appearing of itself: See Key Terms: *tzu-jan*.

38   **Duty:** In Confucian social philosophy, Duty *(yi)* is the ability to apply the prescriptions of Ritual (see below) in specific situations. See my translation of *The Analects*, p. 248.

Ritual: In Confucian social philosophy, Ritual *(li)* is the sacred web of social responsibilities that bind a society together. See my translation of *The Analects*, pp. xxii ff. & 247.

60   **Govern . . . fish:** That is: as if it were an insignificant matter, and with the least handling possible.

spirits . . . ghosts: It was generally believed that a person's "spirit" normally thins away shortly after death. But if a person dies an unnatural death, the "spirit" was thought to become an enduring "ghost" which haunts the living world causing trouble.

69   **treasures:** See section 67.

74   **the Executioner:** Variously identified as *tzu-jan*, heaven, the Way of heaven, or Way itself.

79   **half of contracts:** Signed contracts were torn in half and each party kept one side as proof of the agreement.

·

Key Terms
An Outline of Lao Tzu's Thought

Tao: 道 Way

As the generative ontological process through which all things arise and pass away, Tao might provisionally be divided into being (the ten thousand things of the empirical world in constant transformation) and nonbeing, the generative source of being and its transformations. See also: Introduction pp. x and xvi.

Ref: *passim.*

Te: 德 Integrity

Integrity to Tao in the sense of "abiding by the Way," or "enacting the Way." Hence, it is Tao's manifestation in the world, especially in a sage master of Tao. See also: Introduction p. xxiii.

Ref: *passim.*

Tzu-jan: 自然 Occurrence appearing of itself

The ten thousand things unfolding spontaneously from the generative source, each according to its own nature. Hence, *tzu-jan* might be described as the mechanism or process of Tao in the empirical world. See also: Introduction pp. xx ff.

Ref: 17.9, 23.1, 25.22, 51.8, 64.27.

Wu-wei: 無爲 Nothing's own doing, etc.

Impossible to translate the same way in every instance, *wu-wei* means acting as a spontaneous part of *tzu-jan* rather than with self-conscious intention. Different contexts emphasize different aspects of this rich philosophical concept as Lao Tzu exploits the term's grammatical ambiguity. Literally meaning "not/nothing *(wu)* doing *(wei),*" *wu-wei's* most straightforward translation is simply "doing nothing" in the sense of not interfering with the flawless and self-sufficient unfolding of *tzu-jan.* But this must always be conceived together with its mirror translation: "nothing doing" or "nothing's own doing," in the sense of being no one separate from *tzu-jan* when acting. As *wu-wei* is the movement of *tzu-jan,* when we act according to *wu-wei* we act as the generative source. This opens to the deepest level of this philosophical complex, for *wu-wei* can also be read quite literally as "nonbeing (wu) doing." Here, *wu-wei* action is action directly from, or indeed *as* the ontological source: nonbeing burgeoning forth into being. This in turn invests the more straightforward translation ("doing nothing") with its fullest dimensions, for "doing nothing" always carries the sense of "enacting nothing/nonbeing." See also: Introduction pp. xxiii ff.

> Ref: 2.11, 3.12, 10.8, 37.1, 38.5, 43.3 & 5, 47.8, 48.4-5, 57.15, 63.1, 64.15.

T'ien   天 Heaven

The Chou Dynasty used the impersonal concept of heaven to replace the Shang Dynasty's monotheistic god. Heaven was eventually secularized by the early Taoists, Lao Tzu and Chuang Tzu, for whom it meant natural process: the constant unfolding of things in the cosmological process. For a somewhat different perspective, consider the recurring entity "heaven and earth," which might be conceived as "creative force and created objects." See also: Introduction pp. xiv and xix–xx.

> Ref: *passim.*

Hsüan   **玄**   Dark-enigma

Dark-enigma came to have a particular philosophic resonance, for it became the name of a neo-Taoist school of philosophy in the third and fourth centuries C.E.: Dark-Enigma Learning, a school which gave Chinese thought a decidedly ontological turn and became central to the synthesis of Taoism and Buddhism into Ch'an Buddhism. Like Lao Tzu, the thinkers of the DarkEnigma Learning school equated dark-enigma with nonbeing, the generative ontological tissue from which the ten thousand things spring. Or more properly, it is Way before it is named, before nonbeing and being give birth to one another – that region where consciousness and ontology share their source.

Ref: 1.9-10, 6.2-3, 10.5-6, 15.2, 51.17, 56.9, 65.11-12.

Mu, etc.   **母**   Mother, etc.

The philosophy of Tao embodies a cosmology rooted in that most primal and wondrous presence: earth's mysterious generative force. This represents a resurgence of the cosmology of late Paleolithic and early Neolithic cultures, where this force was venerated as the Great Mother. She continuously gives birth to all creation, and like natural process which she represents, she also takes life and regenerates it in an unending cycle of life, death, and rebirth. In the *Tao Te Ching*, this awesome generative force appears most explicitly in Lao Tzu's recurring references to the female principle in a variety of manifestations: mother, female, feminine, yielding, source, origin, etc. But in the end, it is everywhere in the *Tao Te Ching*, for it is nothing other than Tao itself. See also: Introduction pp. ix-x and *passim*.

Ref: 1.3-4, 4.3-4, 6.1-3, 10.9, 14.20, 19.10, 20.29, 21.15-16, 25.6, 28.2, 42.1f, 51.1&9&14, 52.1-6, 59.10, 61.3-4, 70.5.